Poetry or Just Life

by
Gladys Lois Felder Washington

Edelweiss Publishers
Anderson, South Carolina

Copyright ©2023 by Gladys Lois Felder Washington
Cover design and book interior layout by Genie Ross
Cover and interior art by Frankie O. Felder
Book production by Asya Blue Design
Edited by Frankie O. Felder

All rights reserved. In accordance with the U.S. Copyright Act of 1976, the scanning, uploading, and electronic sharing of any part of this book without proper written permission of the author constitute unlawful theft of the author's intellectual property.

ISBN paperback 978-1-7363779-3-2

Poetry

Edelweiss Publishers, Anderson, South Carolina
Printed in the United States of America 2023
Minuteman Press, Anderson, South Carolina

DEDICATION

For my paternal grandmother, Beatrice O. Felder, educator and private school founder, who instilled a love of reading and personal writings in her children and future generations;

For my father, Tyree P. Felder, who passed along the gift of writing and poetry to his children through bedtime stories he often read to us;

For my sisters, Frankie, Deborah, Marva and Tyrelle, and stepmother, Muriel, who give me plenty of reasons to look at life through the eyes of a poet;

For my husband, Lloyd G. Washington, who as a poet in his own right, captured my heart;

For my children, Ayse, Tasha, and N'Gai, and my dearest friends and extended family who have tolerated my ramblings and encouraged me through the years to gather my scattered poems and compile this collection.

Thanks to poetry, I hope I have a positive legacy that my children and grandchildren will appreciate. May they share my love of poetry when life is a little challenging. Maybe they'll read something that I wrote and see life as I do – just poetry.   ~ Gladys

INTRODUCTION

Poetry. The word alone often makes people cringe. They say they do not like it at all and would never sit to read a poem or, heaven forbid, memorize one. Interesting. I do not think there is a person alive who has not been introduced to poetry, even from the womb. Our mothers sang to us before we were born. We hear music throughout our lives. Even music without words brings us visions of something familiar, something warm, something pleasant, something happy or even something sad.

Life itself is poetry. Everything we see is a poem, if we think about it. Whether in prose or rhythmic and metered, poetry conveys a message and elicits human feelings. We all share these same feelings from time to time and thus we share poetry. Poems speak to us individually and interpretation of any poem is very personal. I cannot tell you what a poem will mean to you. I cannot tell you what a poem I read twenty years ago meant to me then or if I will have that same interpretation or feeling about it if I were to read it again today. Poetic interpretation is affected by experience and age.

As I have learned to experience life through my poetry, I have also learned to use poetry as a mode of therapy – cheaper than shopping or an analyst! It is often cleansing and can simultaneously be fun. Just as other artists create their crafts, poets find that words may flow effortlessly and frequently or may struggle to eradicate a dry spell or complete a thought. Regardless, I have found that poetry, like music ". . . hath charms to soothe a savage breast. To soften rocks or bend the knotted oak." (William Congreve, 1697, *The Morning Bride*.)

CONTENTS

Aging, 1-18
Aging with Grace
Eighty
Feeble
Gather Joy
Hands of Time
Hickory Dickory Dock
Lines of My Face
On Turning Thirty
Weekend
When

Departing, 19-31
As I Leave You
Eternal Peace
I Bring You Back
Living 'Midst the Rain
No More Tears
Respectable Period of Mourning
Seasons
Tomorrow
Wait

Family, 33-55
A Mother's Vindication
By Intention
Happy Birthday
His Flowers
His Heart
I Am Because They Were
Like Sisters
Not Just a Daughter-in-Law
Sisters
Sisters of Mine

Tear-Soaked Soil
Their H-I-S-t-o-r-y
Tiny Little Baby
To My Son(s)
Wait! What? Another Sister!

God and Christmas, 57-90
Again The Christmas Season
Ain't You Shame?
Christmases
How Could We Ask for More?
Humanity
Lost at Christmas
No Christmas Tree
No Truer Gifts
Not That Serious
Nothing is More Precious
Peace for Sleep
So Jesus Won't be Sad
Step by Step
The Christmas Breakfast
The Christmas Magic
The Christmas Mantra
The Christmas Me I Am
We Don't Know
When Came that Christmas Day
When You Believe

Life, 91-126
A Caregiver's Prayer
Changes
Cry a River
Daddy's Footsteps
Day by Day
How You Make Me Feel
I Smile
I'm Only a Machine

Let Me Borrow Your Husband
Mekhi and the Sea Turtle
Night Flight
Ode to a Mouse
One More Day
Pity Party
Remembered So
Rescued
Tale of a Puppy's Tail
Three Rings
Today is a Good Day . . . A Friend Responds

Love and Friendship, 127-148
Always Here
Appropriate
Emotion
For You Have Seen
Friend
If Time Stood Still
Proclivity Component
Should I?
The Care Package
The Gladiola
The Single Tear
Until
You Don't
Your Eyes
Your Star

About the Author, 149

AGING . . .

Aging with Grace
Eighty
Feeble
Gather Joy
Hands of Time
Hickory Dickory Dock
Lines of My Face
On Turning Thirty
Weekend
When

AGING WITH GRACE

Let me age with a little grace
With silver hair in proper styles
Keep soft the lines that mar the face
And tell of traveled miles.

Let me age with a little grace
Showing others what to do
When they with time cannot keep pace
And aging catches them, too.

Let me age with just enough grace
That when youngsters upon me view
Their own subtle changes they'll embrace
Seeing aging with eyes anew.

12/03/2009

EIGHTY

One day when I am eighty
And my hair is all in gray
I hope to look just half as good
As you look to me today!

I hope that I am straight and tall
With skin that hides my age
I'd like to keep them guessing
While they try to count my grays.

I hope that I am sharp of mind
And know all that's going on
No one could surprise or fool me
After living quite that long!

I hope my tongue, like yours, is sharp
And can challenge Webster's English
With words like "como se llama"
"Caramba" and "circumsquelish."

I hope my friends and family
Will all want to be there
When I am turning eighty
Just to show how much they care!

So now that you are eighty
And see all your life has meant
Remember that to be so loved
Shows a life that was well spent.

I'll use you as an example
To follow my life through
So that everyone will love me
The way that they love you.

May I just be so lucky
To live to see that day
When I have achieved eighty
And my hair is all in gray.

By Gladys and Lloyd Washington

Dedicated to Benjamin Canute Washington for his eightieth birthday

11/1991

FEEBLE

Today when I got out of bed
And looked into my mirror
"I'm getting old," to me I said
A thought that made me quiver.

I should have known right then and there
The kind of day it would be
My usual drive wrought with despair
Not feeling quite like me.

"Now never mind, aren't you alive?"
Says I to me while dressing
Then brushed my teeth with VO5
And ran my last pair of stockings.

"Call in sick, I do implore!"
A voice somewhere insisted
I heeded not, tripped through the door
And found my ankle twisted.

Expletives began to flow
In rapid, muted succession
From whence I'm sure I do not know
(*If asked at next confession*).

Enough time lost, I'd work to do
So I hobbled to my car
I couldn't just sit there and stew
The office wasn't that far.

Then things began to go my way
My tape deck playing *Johnny*
Light traffic for that time of day
The weather clear and sunny.

Then when I reach the parking lot
My choice of spaces making
Someone was *always* in my spot
But today NO space was taken.

A feeble thought began to lurk
This wasn't even funny . . .
The roads were clear; no one at work . . .
OH, EXPLETIVE! IT'S SUNDAY!

3/3/1992

GATHER JOY

70 years you've spent on the earth
Busy with life's many chores
Building all that you are worth
Acquiring all that's yours.

70 years you've gathered friends
Your family is strong and true
Your trophies measure many tens
Your regrets measure few.

70 years some say is old
But they're too young to know
This is the time to show you're bold
And there's still time to grow.

70 years show what you've done
Don't let life throw you a ploy
You've yet another race to run
So go and gather joy!

Be blessed in your 7th decade.

12/8/2018

HANDS OF TIME

I'm being whipped – by the hands of time,
But the hands, they just don't care.
Restless, tossing all night long
And wrinkles forming everywhere.

I've tried to stop those ruthless hands,
To turn them back just a bit.
With creams and potions and magic pills
But those hands, they just will not quit.

So here sit I in midnight's gloom,
Not awake, but neither asleep.
Too hot, then too cold with no control
While those hands continue their sweep.

What care give they, to the harsh dismay
Of the loss of my youthful look,
To the sun-dried hands and the sagging face
Not recognized by a glancing look?

They know no mercy, those hands of time.
They do not heed my pleads.
I once grabbed those hands to force them back
And was dragged to my weakening knees.

Some say that, "It's just plain aging,
You can't stop it . . . don't you know?
Don't waste your time and good earned money
Give in and just go with the flow."

So what if your assets are sagging,
Moving further south with each passing day?
So what if your veins look like rivers
That dried up and sank in the clay?

So what if your hair, now gray and thinning,
Has lost volume and luster with time?
So what if you can't remember what you just said,
As easily as you did in your prime?

So what if you name all your children
Before you call the one that you mean?
So what if they laugh as you struggle to stand
And on some stick you now have to lean?
Haven't you earned the right to these milestones?
Haven't you worked all your life to get here?
To this place that's not all that familiar
Full of uncertainty, solitude, and fear?

I mean, your friends and your loved ones are dwindling
As fast as the hairs leave your head.
You gave up rich foods, then liquid libations
For gluten-free, dairy-free and meat-free instead.

There's no truth that's truer than time passage,
So, face it . . . or ignore as you will.

Not crying, nor begging, nor potions
Can halt your descent down that hill.

Oh sure, some slide slower than others!
But down that steep slope we'll all go.
But know, if I get there before you,
I'll be there to soften your blow.

Don't dismay and wind up foolhardy!
Don't throw in the towel and accept it!
With pride, shake those hands as they pass by
Declaring you weren't made to quit.

You've smiled to greet a new morning,
No matter how little you slept.
The sun warmed your face with a new day,
As over you, time's hands have swept.

Gladly move onward with gratitude
If your step be your own or be caned,
Or if you just sit and smell roses,
Enjoy all those changes you've gained.

Be thankful time's hands are still passing.
Your age-marks sing of verses you've sung,
Of wisdom that only time bestows,
But never on those who are young.

3/12/2021

HICKORY DICKORY DOCK

Hickory dickory dock

There's something wrong with my clock

Three kids went to bed

But adults got up instead

Hickory dickory dock.

Hickory dickory dock

With my glasses I can't read this clock

I feel twenty-two

But, my mirror says, "Not true!"

Hickory dickory dock.

Hickory dickory dock

You know what to do with this clock...?!

There are face-lifts and tucks

And for a few bucks

I can look just as good as I feel!

11/1997

LINES OF MY FACE

My beauty is on another plain
Not measured by the sum of my parts.
My beauty shines from my soul and mind
And the goodness that's here in my heart.

My legs may not be long or shapely
It's been said I have horrible eyes.
My form was not built like a pinup
My body is a clever disguise.

It guards me from those who are shallow
From those who just like glitter and show.
My body weeds out all the rascals
And protects the me they'll never know.

You'll know me beyond merely vision
Far beyond all the lines of my face.
You'll know me by my deeds and actions
You'll know me by my poise and grace.

To me it means it will not matter
That gravity my parts may displace.
You saw far beyond parts that flatter
And beyond all the lines of my face.

11/1998

ON TURNING THIRTY

We were there when you were born
Could not have missed it for the world
Surprised on your arrival
You avoided being a girl.

Right then you broke tradition
Doing everything your way
You nearly drove us both mad
From your birth to this very day.

Today as you turn thirty
And our hair grows grey and thin
Keep marching to your own tune
True to your spirit deep within.

Remember that we love you
No matter how tough life gets
Stay on the path God shows you
For a long life without regrets.

Happy Birthday and Every Day
With much love, Mom and Dad

12/20/2008

WEEKEND

Well so today is Friday
And the calendar says Thirteen
And so what if it's October
And you think of Halloween.

The air is warm and humid
The leaves are not yet brown
It's still summer in South Florida
Lose that superstitious frown.

Corporate's busy working
On the things that they do best
Billing, plotting, planning
Putting your patience to the test.

Just be glad today is Friday
Don't whine, or hide or bawl
Throw some salt over your shoulder
It's the weekend after all!

10/13/1989

When . . . ?

When I'm full of more vim than of vigor
When my bark is far worse than my bite
When my glasses can't fix my poor vision
When I finally lose all eyesight

When I answer to questions not asked me
When I don't hear each word that you say
When my knees fail me in walking
When from home I confusedly stray

When I can't remember my intentions
When I wear two shoes that don't match
When I put my underwear over my clothes
When you touch me, I fight, bite and scratch

When you leave me alone, I get frightened
When you come back, I don't know who you are
When you give me a set of fake keys
When I think I can still drive the car

When I forget how to feed myself
When my makeup is all out of place
When I answer the door and there's nobody there
When I'm never in my own space

When you greet me and I've lost my smile
When my body is aching and broken
When my posture shows miles without grace
When at last, no more words are spoken . . .

Will you in fondness remember?
Will you care for me, as I did you?
And when that time finally comes
Will you let me go as you must do?

1/11/2018

Departing...

As I Leave You
Eternal Peace
I Bring You Back
Living 'Midst the Rain
No More Tears
Respectable Period of Mourning
Seasons
Tomorrow
Wait

AS I LEAVE YOU

Grieve not for me as I leave you
I've been gone now for quite some time
It is I who must offer condolence
For you who I leave here behind.

My Father has beckoned me to Him
To shed all my anguish and pain
He offers me refuge and comfort
That I've prayed for time and again.

Grieve not for me as I leave you
It's a journey I've planned for so long
My spirit is free of this body
So praise Him and thank Him with song.

As I close my eyes for this last time
My thoughts are for those left behind
A prayer for their repose and solace
And some words that may give peace of mind.

Grieve not for me as I leave you
My purpose on earth now fulfilled
So, I'm resting at home with my Father
And I'll wait for you there as He willed.

7/3/1996

ETERNAL PEACE

The eyes have closed
The body rests
The fight well fought – now over.
The strength once gone
Is now restored
As he lay down in clover.

The life was lived
He touched and loved
Some undertakings achieved.
His time too short
But celebrate
The man he tried to be.

So mourn him not
For he's not there
Where you lay him in the ground.
No more to bear
That body frail
HIS eternal peace he's found.

For Rohan

9/1/2009

I BRING YOU BACK

I HAVE COME TO BRING YOU BACK

TO YOUR SKY, YOUR SEA, YOUR EARTH

TO YOUR LAND OF MANY PEOPLE

TO YOUR BELOVED LAND OF BIRTH.

I BRING YOU BACK THIS LAST TIME

FOREVER TO BE A PART

OF THE PLACE YOU NEVER REALLY LEFT . . .

TOO EMBEDDED DEEP IN YOUR HEART.

SO GO NOW TO YOUR LAND AND SEA

YOUR SKY SO BRIGHT, SO BLUE

AND KNOW THAT AS I LEAVE YOU HERE

A PART OF ME STAYS, TOO.

11/18/2012

LIVING 'MIDST THE RAIN

Nature came before us
On this, man must agree
Each element most sustaining
Earth and sky and sea.

The body and the spirit
Exist by grand design
And pass through this dimension
On a course unsure and fine.

We wonder of life's purpose
Searching answers we can't know
Of why we've even come here
And when or how we'll go.

We live with expectations
Going on from day to day
With hopes for more tomorrows
In sunshine without rain.

Yet rains do interrupt us
And it's then that we reflect
On purpose and on meaning
On life with circumspect.

Heavy rains bring heavy hearts
For our losses we will pine
Yet all things, only lent to us,
Through love's memory still will shine.

For we came from the Creator
To the Creator we'll return
This life and our travel partners
Are only lessons we must learn.

So, when the rains surround you
And heavy clouds upon you drain
Know God sends His loving sunshine
To sustain you 'midst the rain.

10/22/2017

NO MORE TEARS

The chariot's door has opened wide
To carry his spirit back home
He's freed from the chains of his body
That kept him away from the throne.

We mourn for ourselves at his leaving
Forgetting the plan is divine
That our lives are but for a moment
Before we leave others behind.

Blessed are we to have had the privilege
To be sons and daughters or friends
'Fore he names us to The Almighty
That we might be with him again.

Without words he said he was ready
His hand gently beckoned me near
His eyes smiled and gave me his message
Don't cry now – "Just be of good cheer."

Though reddened and swollen our eyes cry
Our hearts by his memory are fed
In glory he lives with The Father
So, no tears for him should we shed.

12/4/2000

Respectable period of mourning

Time to get up and be who you are
And not the you, you used to be
High time to move on and go where you're drawn
Forsaking past ghosts, you must flee.

Though pleasant and vast, those memories past
They jealously hold you in place
Remaining here still, exerting their will
It's you who denies them their space.

For as they did say, past is the day
Respectfully mourned is their passing
Obligations all met, voided by death
Their love for you still everlasting.

Hold not onto things that hold back your dreams
Retarding your waking and living
It may be six weeks, six months or six years
When release to yourself you'll be giving.

The decision but yours, to open new doors
For your actions your lover's not scoring
That time they'll respect, for it's yours to set –
That "respectable period of mourning."

Rest in peace, my dear husband.
Lloyd George Washington (7/16/1947 – 3/23/2012)

1/6/2018

SEASONS

In seasons of the sunny sky
Our hearts are light and gay
Forgetting rains are surely nigh
And great sorrows will flood that day.

In bright sunshine and in morning rain
With the smell of fresh soaked grass
The tiny buds of spring regain
Their strength to rise at last.

The moon beams bring reflection . . .
Quiet time to contemplate
On our gifts and God's protection
When life's trials our souls frustrate.

Since our seasons, unrevealed to us,
Start and end without consent
We must live each day as precious
The way our Father meant.

Coming seasons have their reasons
Ponder not what or when or why
For as surely as the day we're born
The day comes when we'll die.

So live and laugh and love boldly;
Do a daily kindness to mankind.
Lift a heart that may be lonely;
Avoid words that will malign.

Now in this season of our grief –
Rejoice for the knowing of
the life whose season was far too brief –
But never too short on love.

For Yvette

4/18/2019

TOMORROW

We don't have tomorrow
And the past is but a yesterday
There is but this one moment
In which to praise and pray.

You need not be down on your knees
To do the Father's will
Just reach out to your brothers
And praise God through your skill.

I came to you a broken man
My needs both great and small
You sang, or prayed, or picked me up
Whenever I did call.

You tended to my fish tanks
You mowed my weed-filled lawn
You rescued my financial needs . . .
My soul felt no forlorn.

For that, no words can thank you
You carried me through my end
It's been my greatest pleasure
That you were my true friend.

Though we don't have tomorrows
We have had wonderful yesterdays
So share your gifts with your brothers
For love has no truer measure
Than the gifts that it displays.

A final message to my friends. Lloyd Washington

3/23/2012

WAIT

Why brings us tears – the loss of life?
It is the way intended
By which concludes our earthly strife
And all souls to God ascended.

So, celebrate the passing on
Be free of death's deception
For in our dying, we are born
Our Maker's chief intention.

Free your hearts from pain and fear
Death, too, shall be our fate.
We'll keep the joyous memories dear
And live just to pass the wait.

11/2000

FAMILY . . .

A Mother's Vindication
By Intention
Happy Birthday
His Flowers
His Heart
I Am Because They Were
Like Sisters
Not Just a Daughter-in-Law
Sisters
Sisters of Mine
Tear-Soaked Soil
Their H-I-S-t-o-r-y
Tiny Little Baby
To My Son(s)
Wait! What? Another Sister!

A MOTHER'S VINDICATION

For all the cold rejection
Of your teaching what to do
A mother's vindication comes
When kids start to act like you.

They swear they'll never do or say
The things their mothers did
Then one day when they've gone away
And are no longer just your kid
Some little thing your tried to teach
'Till you were turning blue
Lets you know that you did reach
That brain they hid from view.

What better vindication
For the stress they put you through
Than when kids start to realize
How much they are like you!

5/5/1996

BY INTENTION

I came when not expected
It may not have been your plan
To be so small and needy
But I'm doing what I can.

I may not have all the parts
That the other babies do
I'll use the parts God gave me
And you'll see how I get through.

So don't worry about me
God sent me on a mission
It's just between Him and me
I'll see it to fruition.

Not before my task is done
Will He call me to come home
Your job is just to love me
And know I'm not here alone.

My angels are here with me
They are guiding all I do
So praise Him and be grateful
For the time I'm here with you.

I may be here a short while
Or way after you are gone
If I told you the true plan
That would make our lives all wrong.

My life is by intention
I've a purpose to fulfill
I'll not leave 'till it's completed
Because that is by His will.

So though this was not your plan
In case I failed to mention
Long or short, normal or not,
My life Is by intention!

I Love You Mom and Dad.
Miley Liane Clarke

7/3/2014

HAPPY BIRTHDAY

I may have missed your party
Didn't get a piece of cake
But couldn't let the day go by
Without this wish to make

A day that's full of laughter
A week that's full of fun
A month that brings some extra time
To enjoy being twenty-one (*again*)!

1/7/2004

HIS FLOWERS

May God's angels bless your new home
And all those who dwell therein
May they guard each of your travels
To bring you home safe again.

May you stop to count His blessing
As you kneel each night to pray
Make the time to smell His flowers
When he wakes you every day.

2/14/1998

HIS HEART

His heart is broken and so is mine
A fatal flaw I've made
He couldn't feel the love I gave
From the time he was a babe.

Working daily to give him comforts
And the things I didn't have
I failed to see the emptiness . . .
The distance growing wide.

I let him down when he needed me most
My babe turning into a man
He no longer sat upon my lap
But he still needed to hold my hand.

How do I talk to this grown man
All filled with so much pain
How do I reach his heart and soul
And bring him home again?

We may not always agree
On situations great or small
I need to let him know somehow
He's my own son after all.

No force on earth can change that
He's my flesh and blood and sweat
I did what I thought best for him
To spare him from life's regrets.

If you thought somehow I failed you
If you never knew I tried
If you thought you weren't important
If you ever felt I lied . . .

As a man now with new insights
Gained by lessons taught from this earth
Can you not see where your heart is
And where your soul finds its true mirth?

I appeal to your higher senses
To the intelligence you've gained
I appeal to your "man in the mirror"
To see your thoughts that have you chained.

My arms are always open
My heart more open still
So open now your broken heart
And let those child wounds heal.

Every mother to her son

11/30/2022

I AM BECAUSE THEY WERE

Whatever it is that I am, is not of me alone.
It's that eternal journey from some blood-soaked motherland,
And the survival lessons the ancestors' lives have shown
That bring me to opportunities paid for with shattered hands.

I'll not hang my head in feigned shame;
The shame cannot be mine.
Whether man, woman or child – they withstood each captor's bout.
Tho' skin whipped raw and bleeding, then brutally soaked in brine; their resolve never faltered; those attacks they meant to flout.

They laid down a firm foundation to prosper and to grow,
To use our God-given talents to learn, and build, and till.
To add now to this our nation, this is the least I owe.
With humble appreciation, their steps I'll vow to fill.

This truth, for sure, I won't deny when all is said and done.
Today I am that vision the ancestral slaves did spur.
May their pride, their toils, and their ransom be ignored by none.
I owe a debt I'll always pay; I am because they were.

Written for *OURstory Unchained and Liberated from HIStory* (published 2021)

10/4/2020

LIKE SISTERS

Just as we choose not our ancestry
Sisters are a package deal
But like sisters we have history
Years of sharing now congeal.

Closer than a few by natural birth
I'm pleased to include you in
The limited list of those on earth
I'd choose as my sister or my kin.

You've been my sister in many ways
You cheered me when I was down
Forever you'll hear me sing your praise
You deserve a saintly crown.

So happy wishes, though maybe late
May your fondest dreams come true
Sister, were I there I'd bake this cake
That I've packaged up for you.

1/7/13

NOT JUST A DAUGHTER-IN-LAW

You know you're not my daughter
And never could you be
You're married to that son of mine
Which makes you a part of me.

You don't replace a mother
She'll be ever in your heart
With all her love and memories
That in you she did impart.

But know that you are more to me
Than just a daughter-in-law
We'll always laugh and talk and share
These things I'll not withdraw.

You're fully vested in our lives
A child of mine throughout eternity
So accept this birthday wish I send
With my full sincerity.

Long life with health and peace of mind
Good memories of the past
Contentment knowing your time in space
Is filled with love unsurpassed.
Happy Birthday!

3/6/2016

SISTERS

Most anyone can have a sister
It's not the hardest thing to do
You just sit and wait or ask your parents
And one will probably come to you.

They're often your first playmate
Or someone with whom to fight
Or someone you share a room with
So you're not all alone at night.

They can get you into trouble
Or maybe you've cause them some strife
But no matter the situation
They are your sister all through life.

They are happy when you're happy
They cry when you are sad
And when it comes to Goodwill fashion
They make sure that you're well clad.

When life gets hard (and it sure can)
They know just what you need
A phone call full of laughter
Through which no one can intercede.

You're blessed if you have a sister
One who's always got your back
To share those coded secrets
Watson and Holmes can't even crack.

So thanks for being my sister
Not sure if by my request
But there's no doubt about it
Because of you, Sis, I've been blessed!

To Frankie

12/20/2018

SISTERS OF MINE

I ask you, do you have a sister
One older or younger than you
One who is always under foot
Or one who tells you what to do?

Does she exasperate, defy or question
Every move or decision you make?
Is she forever all up in your business
And your jewelry and clothes she may take?

Does she eavesdrop then tell all your secrets
Does she rat you out to your parents
When questioned about broken items
Or that strange marshmallow disappearance?

Does she give you advice you don't ask for
Does she think all your boyfriends are nerdy
Then tell you to show them the door
Since of your attention they're not worthy?

Does she think that she's always right
Because she finished a class more that you
Does she fact check each word out of your mouth
Because to her that word is new?

Well, what if you, like I, have four sisters
No brothers to soften the strife
You're all alone with these people
Who are with you throughout all your life.

Oh sure, you can squabble and fight
Not speak to them for years on end
But when it comes down to life's trials
Your sisters are there thick and thin.

So be honored that you do have sisters
Never let them get you in a frenzy
If you have one or so many more
It's a gift that brings others to envy.

I cherish the differences of each one
And though we may be far apart
By geography or philosophy
We'll always be sisters at heart.

12/2/22

TEAR-SOAKED SOIL

They came here to be, but not by their wish
To toil and to slave every day
To cook all the food and clean every dish
Then pack all their fine wares away.

Never did they enjoy that fine food
They worked all the lands, but shared not their yields
For them only remnants and spoils
For them only hard work in fields.

But heads held high with saintly pride
Their tears they'd not display
Their strength they carried deep inside
Knowing the future held a better day.

And while they weren't to be free
They kept faith and courage strong
That their children would never see
Conditions so cruel and so wrong.

The tear-soaked soil of the fathers
Has paid for our right to be free
A debt is owed not measured by others
This debt is for you and for me.

We pay with our building and earning
We pay when we do well in school
We pay when we continue our yearning
To engage yet be nobody's fool.

God blessed the tear-soaked soil
That brought us at last to this day
In which we have pride and don't recoil
And let no man again make us prey.

10/4/2020

THEIR *H-I-S*-t-o-r-y

I stand here before you, forefathers,
Bursting with humility and pride
So honored that you came before me
To pattern our course as a guide.

You showed strength in the face of trials
You showed faith when I surely would faint
You lived with conviction and self-respect
Your courage would challenge a saint.

And now I go on in your footsteps
I've learned by the example you gave
Let me honor the courage and wisdom
You showed even though still enslaved.

I'll use my talents and training
I'll show who a slave can create
A doctor, a lawyer and president
Their *H-I-S*-t-o-r-y will not be my fate.

10/4/2020

TINY LITTLE BABY
(A Lullaby for Luke)

Tiny little baby sleeping on my arm
With your mommy and your daddy keeping you from harm.
Sleep and close your little eyes.
Know that Mom and Dad are here.
Now close your eyes and go to sleep.
You'll never have to fear.

Tiny little baby sleeping on my arm
You are just the best of us with all your baby charm.
Don't you know we love you?
We'll always keep you safe.
So, close your eyes and go to sleep,
This is your slumber place.

6/16/2021

TO MY SON(S)

You told me that you loved her
And that you'd always care
You'd protect her and defend her
Your name with her you'd share.

You asked if you could keep her
I told you, "She's not a pet!"
Can't just make a promise
Then casually forget.

Her skin is made of crystal
Her heart bone-china fine
You promised she you'd cherish
Like a fine imported wine.

I said, "Son, let me tell you
What you're asking is for life
The day you promise, "I Do"
And take her as your wife.

To protect her and defend
Means you'll always put her first
Broken crystal you can't mend
And a heart can die from thirst!"

So now you are deciding
The man you're going to be
You're loving and supporting
A wife and family.

Of greater still importance
On you she must depend
Her knight in shining armor
Who'll love, protect, defend.

Life's not a bed of clover
All those house chores must be done
It looks like playtime's over
A man's job is not all fun.

Be wise! Be smart! Be loving!
Be the man who makes her proud
Those will meet her expectations
To place you above the crowd.

12/25/03

WAIT! WHAT? ANOTHER SISTER!

I already have a sister
A brother's what I need
I'm sure I put in my request
A brother, please, I'd plead!

But then the day you came home
Cute as a button and oh so smart
You said exactly what you wanted
You ruled us all right from the start.

We tried to turn you into our dolly
Your other sister and I
Again you said, "No way Jose!"
And began that awful baby cry!

You'd be rescued by our mother
Sometimes Dad stepped in instead
You rudely gave us raspberries
As Sis and I got sent to bed.

With all that it never mattered
You had our hearts from that first day
You were our sister just the same
And with you our hearts will stay.

A sister's better than a brother
No matter if we play or fight
We can share our clothes and secrets
We'll defend you with all our might!

So, wait! What? Today's your birthday?
Time to stop and celebrate
And say we're glad you're our sister
Whether by wish or just plain fate.

Fondu is great with wine and cake
I, too, want so to be there
To give that happy birthday wish
That shows how very much we care.

By Gladys and Frankie for Debbie.

12/22/2020

God and Christmas ...

Again the Christmas Season
Ain't You Shame?
Christmases
How Could We Ask for More?
Humanity
Lost at Christmas
No Christmas Tree
No Truer Gifts
Not that Serious
Nothing Is More Precious
Peace for Sleep
So Jesus Won't be Sad
Step by Step
The Christmas Breakfast
The Christmas Magic
The Christmas Mantra
The Christmas Me I Am
We Don't Know
When Came that Christmas Day
When You Believe

AGAIN THE CHRISTMAS SEASON

The crowds are back, the stores are packed
No parking space to spare
Those doing well are all decked out
For a grand black-tie affair.

Their gifts are wrapped to proper style –
Beneath the tree they lay
Awaiting happy anxious hands
That will wreck the neat display.

Now, did I get that color right?
Is this size too big or small?
I may just have to take it back
If they don't like it at all.

Again the Christmas season
Has turned our thoughts around
Far from the child who started this
Whose name is most renowned.

He came to show us how to live
To have strength and not be faint
To help someone who's down and out
Without payment or complaint.

He didn't bring a pretty gift
From the most respected store
But what He gave to each of us
Should make all our spirits soar.

Pay it forward to your brothers
All the gifts He's strewn on you
Make again the Christmas season
About His love the whole year through.

By Lloyd and Gladys

12/24/2011

AIN'T YOU SHAME?

Santa, Santa, ain't you shame
For all the hoopla that you claim
With EACH and EVERY Christmas?

I mean, the kids are more than hyped
With thoughts of toys every night
And you don't even ask forgiveness!

You know that this is not your day
So, at the very least you should say
Happy birthday, Jesus!

With gifts and paper everywhere
It seems that no one gives a care
About the reason for the season.

Little children, ain't you shame
'Bout missing gifts you still complain
And cry for no good reason?

So, I remind you, one and all
The real reason that he comes to call
Those gifts are to show our gratitude.

Gratitude to the ones we love
For that first love from up above
Given to us all by our Father.

So Santa, Santa, ain't you shame
When the message could not be more plain,
To try to top His biggest gift – you don't need to bother.

The Heavenly Father gave His only Son
To show us how life should be done
So Santa, give back some credit.

You have your place in the season's cheer
With elves and sleigh and your reindeer
Now enjoy it as you spread it.

But Santa, it's the baby's day
To little Jesus we'll always pray
So Santa, don't be shame to share His day.

12/25/2021

CHRISTMASES

One o'clock, two o'clock, three o'clock
then four
The scenes of many Christmases flood back to me once more.

The gaily decorated hearth, the reef that graced the door
The visits of strange relatives I'd never met before.

The kitchen clutter everywhere with bowl and pot and pan
Making someone's favorite meals from scratch and all by hand.

One tree trimmed just for children, several others for the grown-up clan
No presents opened before we ate was always the morning's plan.

The crystal and the china that was used but once a year
The silver polished and placed just so for us to use in fear –

Of breaking or misplacing some great-grandma's plate held dear
Kept little ones all tense and anxious and dulled the Christmas cheer.

As a child, it made no sense to me to fuss and bother so
For the food would soon be eaten, and the relatives would go.

The fireplace, short of embers, would lose its former glow
The gifts would have been opened leaving wrappings out to throw.

Exhausted from
festivities that for days,
nay weeks, commenced
Into a few rushed hours all
those Christmas
"joys" condensed.

With thoughts of all the
purchases through
some credit cards
expensed
Brings a little damper to
the spirit that leaves
one tensed.

So for next year let's
forget all that and
celebrate with reason
Let's honor Him
through more kind acts
that surely, He would
please in.

Let's create a world
with resolution that we
can all believe in
Content to know God's
only Son is the true
purpose of this season.

We can hold dear our
Christmases past, while
making traditions anew
Good cooking that we'll all
enjoy and, yes, maybe a
gift or two.

Let the children enjoy
Santa and Elf on the
Shelf to view
As we teach them all
about Jesus to keep our
Christmases true.

12/23/2019

HOW COULD WE ASK FOR MORE?

A list is always on our minds
Of things we like or don't
Of things we know that we will get
And things we know we won't.

The list keeps changing everyday
We forget and can't keep track
Of those times we should be grateful
'Cause we focus on what's whack.

Now we can name the things we hate
And we're sure you will agree
That if you had to deal with these
You'd feel the same as we.

So let us count them out for you
There's more than three or four
Then you tell us if you agree
That these, you *too*, abhor!

Secrets others say they have
And then say they can't tell
That one is the worst, we think
Our blood just wants to jell.

And what about that guy or gal
Whose always in your face
With breath that makes you want to gag
Or move to outer space.

Then that disgusting cockroach
That made you stub your toe
When you kicked it up against a wall
To strike that fatal blow.

Oh yeah, and even more than that
Those cracked screens on the phones
They cut our fingers or our face
'Cause we can't leave them alone.

We hate it when we're hungry
Especially at night
We hate when it's too quiet
These things are never right.

Did we tell you we hate bunions?
Did we mention Zombies, too?
Did we say that we hate Hell, for sure?
And being hot makes us blue?

We also hate when you look sad
But say that nothing's wrong
Or when you say you'll be right back
Then you're gone so long.

We could say more, and go on and on
But you might think us a bore
Some let us say what we DO like
And then we'll say no more.

The favorite thing we like of all
Is God who loves us most
Who came to us on Christmas Day
With no fanfare and no boast.

He was no fashionista
Never thought of what He'd wear
Didn't spend His time in fancy spas
On manicures and hair.

We thought Him just a baby
But in His cleaver disguise
He came to show that He was God
And how we should live our lives.

So God and Family is all we need
These things top all our favorite lists
Of the things that we like best in life
And without which we can't exist.

We know that you really love us
It doesn't come from a fancy store
With God and you as family
How could we ask for more?
How *could* we ask for more?

Merry Christmas!

Composed collectively by Aaliyah, Benjamin, Madison, Mekhi, Solomon, Steven, and Yohana.

12/24/2015

HUMANITY

Humble when you need me

Ungrateful when you do not

Misguided by uncertainty

Abhorrent of all I've taught.

Naïve to your own blind prejudice

Injurious to those you hate

Tainted by vile maliciousness

Yet begging mercy to change your fate.

9/15/2020

LOST AT CHRISTMAS

The economy is failing
Busting out at all its seams
Spilling wide its very guts
Taking everybody's dreams.

Jobs lost daily by the thousands
Home foreclosures every day
On CNN were churches
People filing in to pray.

Not for their souls they knelt down
Nor for salvation did they shout
But to keep the factories open
And for a big cash bail-out.

It was the Christmas season
Yet sadness filled the air
Lamentations for just reason . . .
Was God's presence anywhere?

How easy just to focus
On the stuff they'd lost or would
And not see those in real need
Or a chance to do them good.

Don't let this time of giving
On spending make you stray
From the purpose of His coming
To us all on Christmas Day.

So now stop and praise God
How e're His name you call
For that which cannot be lost
His unfailing love to all.

12/19/2008

NO CHRISTMAS TREE

That year there was no Christmas tree
No joy, no peace on earth
No symbols seen of the spirit
Sent to them with His birth.

The eve of Christmas found them there
At home, but miles apart
Dim visions for their future
Were lurking in their hearts.

The shopping on a smaller scale
The breakfast menu planned
Off to family obligations
Their feelings not well canned.

Perhaps next year a manger scene
Or star glowing oh so bright
Would remind them of that family
That came to all that night.

Hard times seemed to be flowing
With reminders everyday
They wanted to throw in the towel
For His strength they'd need to pray.

Next year had to be better
A small tree they would display
And make some Christmas spirit
That would hide their real dismay.

We all can have His many gifts
At Christmas and year 'round
Just light one little Christmas tree
His strength will then abound.

12/24/2009

NO TRUER GIFTS

OH HOW I'D LOVE TO GIVE YOU

EXPENSIVE GIFTS BENEATH YOUR TREE

WRAPPED AS A PRETTY PARCEL

WITH AN ELEGANT CARD FROM ME.

BUT MORE THAN ANY PRESENT

IF I HAD THE CONTROL

THERE'D BE GOOD HEALTH AND PROSPERITY

OF HEART AND MIND AND SOUL.

SO SINCE I CANNOT GIVE YOU

GIFTS OF THE MATERIAL KIND

I'LL GIVE TO YOU SOME WISDOM . . .

THE BEST GIFTS I COULD FIND.

KNOW THAT EVERY DAY YOU'RE AWESOME

KNOW THAT EVERY DAY YOU'RE BLESSED

KNOW THAT YOUR EARTHLY FAMILY LOVES YOU

KNOW YOU ARE YOUR HEAVENLY FATHER'S BEST.

MANKIND HAS ALL BEEN GIVEN

HIS GREATEST GIFTS WE CAN'T OUTDO

HIS GRACE, HIS LOVE AND HIS MERCY

TO SUSTAIN US OUR WHOLE LIVES THROUGH.

SO WON'T YOU DO THE SAME FOR ME?

I'LL CHERISH THEM MORE THAN I CAN SHOW

GIVE ME HONOR, LOVE, RESPECT AND YOUR TIME

NO TRUER GIFTS CAN YOU BESTOW.

12/20/2018

NOT THAT SERIOUS
(God's Conversation with Himself)

Got up before there was a dawn
Just to make a world for you
Your love for Me would be forgone
As oceans, lands and stars in numbers grew.

Creating for beings I would conceive
My hosts thought too delirious
For man would make all heaven grieve
Taking life as "not that serious."

I knew the plan and saw it clearly
For mankind who would rule the earth
The gifts of life he'd love so dearly . . .
My creation would prove its worth.

And yet, the gift of man's free will
Showed My hosts' concerns had merit
Man's faithless sinning continued until
My heart could no longer bear it.

My plans to prosper and grow his life
He shunned with actions most imperious
Neglecting My warnings to avoid strife
His defiance said life's "not that serious."

The hosts said, "Why not destroy man?
Of your gifts he's not deserving
He doesn't meet your fine, grand plan
All his actions are self-serving."

So to earth, through love, I sent My son
As a babe to whom they'd relate
To save their souls from the defiant one
And to lift life's heavy weight.

All My teachings through that Holy Child
Showed you how to live each day
With faith in Him and evil reviled . . .
Now mercies for your souls you pray.

Alas, today I can celebrate, too,
Failed victory o'er evil most deleterious
Through Christ's teachings you've learned and finally know
That your salvation *is* really that serious.

12/23/2019

NOTHING IS MORE PRECIOUS

In the dawn of your morning
When My thoughts are all on you
I see My great creation
And the things you're meant to do.

Such promise and potential
What great gifts I did impart
Yet used to your destruction
Distressing My hallowed heart.

Now a tear wells in My eyes
Brought forth by your little faith
And callous cold apathy
As your fellow man you scathe.

Should I treat you as you do others
With such narcissistic disregard
I'd hear weeping, moaning and wailing
While pleading for the mercy of God!

This year's blights, long predicted
Should surely not you confound
Now earnestly – just cry out
For I always can be found.

My love of you – eternal
My gifts to you still gracious
My commands say – "Love All Men"
For nothing is more precious.

11/26/2020

PEACE FOR SLEEP

Give me a peace, Lord,
To sleep through this night
To lay down the troubles
I hold to so tight.

God, it's so noisy inside of my head
It rattles with hopes, plans and dreams
As I wonder why there's no sleep in my bed
While I ponder on meaningless things.

You said not to worry – you'd work it all out
Providing each thing I would need
If only I'd let you and lay down my doubt
And daily upon your word feed.

God in heaven up above
Please watch over the ones I love
Help me wake when night is through
To do the things you want me to.

The peace you've given unto me
Is all I need to help bring me sleep
No worried thoughts will I make
And sleep in peace until I wake.

2/1974

. . . SO JESUS WON'T BE SAD

Little children everywhere
Forget what Christmas means
They think of only Santa Claus
And all the gifts he brings.

They pout and display tantrums
When they don't get their way
No thoughts of the little Baby
That was born upon that day.

The Moms and Dads capitulate
They cater to the whims
Of over-privileged children
With wildly flailing limbs.

Again the Christmas Season
Becomes the gimme-gimme time
It's all about what I can get
Or what ought to be mine.

This is the birthday of Jesus
What could His present be?
He cannot open one single gift
That's laid beneath that tree.

I know what you can give Him
It would surely make Him smile
If you were kind to others
And behaved for a little while.

Now just try not to fuss or fight
Show respect for Mom and Dad
Learn to live by the Golden Rule
So Jesus won't be sad.

By Lloyd and Gladys
Especially for all the little ones . . .

12/24/2011

STEP BY STEP

One foot before the other
Step by step they came
Some to sing His praises
Others to blaspheme His name.

How could they know His kingdom
Was not of the things on earth?
How could they see His majesty
In such a humble birth?

Despite heralds of angles
Too few could hardly believe
This tiny little baby
Would the souls of man reprieve.

Step by step He grew wiser
Led by His father's commands
They soon would call Him "Master"
As His words spread through the lands.

All those who sought to shame Him
Only served to fuel the flame
That spread His message further
And immortalized His name.

They tried to kill His body
And secure it in a tomb
Which only healed His spirit
As when nurtured in the womb.

Step by step in Your shadow
I wish to follow Your lead
And light the path for others
As they also are in need.

I pray for You to hear me
I beg pardons I've not gained
I pray step by step for guidance
'Till Your kingdom comes again.

12/20/2020

THE CHRISTMAS BREAKFAST

Christmas Day had come at last
Excitement filled the air
The halls were decked in finery
And children everywhere.

The table held the best display
Of what the world could give
Crystal from some foreign place
Imported is how to live!

Gifts to give and some to get
All carefully selected
Every name was on the list
No one would be neglected.

Of all the treasures well received
One not found in shopping carts
Just a simple gift of love
Christmas breakfast from our hearts.

12/2012

THE CHRISTMAS MAGIC

The magic of Christmas is not a lie
It's true if you want it to be
It gives you joy and a child-like wonder
It's a time when your spirit is free.

The magic began with the baby
When the angels gave Mary the plan
A gift from the Father was coming
To be the salvation of man.

No one believed in that magic
No way could that story be true
That a king would be sent from heavens
And worshiped and followed by few.

But magic did come just as foretold
With the birth of that Heavenly Child
His lessons still taught to this very day
Continue to keep millions beguiled.

Then others did follow His guidance
To give love and their good fortune to share
And we carry on still the tradition
With glad tidings to men everywhere.

So tell me if that isn't magic
If gift giving once a year is a farce
Because childlike wonder's discouraged
World kindness and love is so sparse.

So do I believe in the magic
Of the Christ Child and Santa and elves?
We'd do better to keep any magic
That brings joy to mankind and ourselves.

Join with me to encourage the season
Of excitement in mangers and bright lights
Let's all just believe in the magic
Then watch how spirits can soar to new heights.

12/2/22

THE CHRISTMAS MANTRA

I *hate* Christmas – as you know
All that decking halls and stuff
And cheery salutations
By many just a bluff.

We really ought to just be glad
To live the lives we lead
Giving our love and peace to men
By helping those in need.

"Tis the season to be jolly"
Or so the psalmists say
Glad tidings and good will should be
Our mantra every day.

So, Tasha, as you end this year
Into another go
With our wish that He continues
His blessings on you bestow.

All our love for every season
And just for no good reason

Mom and Dad

12/25/2008

THE CHRISTMAS ME I AM

The sun is rising, so am I
Good thoughts all fill my head
My heart racing with excitement
I bound out of my bed.

The tree, grandiloquent with jewels,
Stands tall to say to all
"Share the best you have with others
Like the babe in the manger stall."

Kind words to all I meet today
Please, thank you, Sir or Ma'am
And let me get that chair for you . . .
That's the Christmas me I am.

The season will soon be over
No trees with lights we'll see
Back to my ordinary life
And back to being me.

My chores I'll do just when I'm told
And not a minute more
For Christmas time has come and passed
So who is keeping score?

When I got up from the table
No one was there to see
And just because I was able
I took my dish with me.

I noticed that one afternoon
A mom with her little baby
Struggling to get through a door
So guess who helped that lady?

It happened almost every day . . .
Deeds I'd not intended
Were done before I thought them through
And they made me feel quite splendid!

Then I remembered Christmas time
And deeds I did just then
Thinking only of my presents
Again and again and again!

Now I know that in every day
I can bring joy to every man
Simply by being my best self
And the Christmas me I am.

12/25/2014

WE DON'T KNOW

We don't know, nor do we need to
If we will see tomorrow
We don't know if we can see through
The things in life that bring us sorrow.

We think that no one knows us
We shield most of who we are
For we only share just what we must
To protect our souls from scars.

We don't know who may be enemies
They may conceal as a dear friend
Who could lead us to calamities
And destruction in the end.

But there is one who knows all
And the roads that we should take
The things we'll do both big and small
And when we're being true or fake.

Choose your friends with some discernment
Guard your words and actions so
Insure against eternal torment
Since His coming we don't know.

1/19/2021

WHEN CAME THAT CHRISTMAS DAY

It was a long and lonely life
That brought me to this place
Where words and deeds unrecognized
Showed in shame upon my face.

Quick to anger and to blame
The onus never mine
'Till what I loved and cherished most
Was all but lost and left behind.

Then the Father did forgive me
For His words I did not heed
For His guidance and correction
That I thought I did not need.

Life moved on as it must do
No season comes to stay
Feeling low and somehow quite alone
Then came *that* Christmas Day

When I knew the Father loved me
For His heart ached with my own pain
Surely lost and unforgiven
'Till came *that* Christmas Day.

He sacrificed His very best
Sending a gift I can't repay
I knew I'd never be alone
When came *that* Christmas Day.

Now let us do our little part
To honor Him this way
With peace and love and forgiveness for all
Because of *that* Christmas Day.

12/2017

WHEN YOU BELIEVE

Jingle Bells, Santa Clause and reindeer deck the Halls
Mistletoe, festive lights, caroling and snow.
Busy shoppers everywhere and traffic at a crawl
Wrapping gifts and taking care to make that perfect bow.

Checking lists, not once, but twice, 'less someone be excluded
Cooking, laundry, cleaning, too, then sending cards
To those social media has eluded.
These are the thoughts at Christmas that the world most regards.

No volcanoes, rains or epic floods could change the hearts of man
So, God, Himself, came down to earth to show us just what mattered.
Through the perfect love of a little child, God would reveal His plan.
By trusting and believing Him our fears and doubts He's shattered.

It's not the gift you got or didn't that should absorb your thought
Or what you wish that you could give to all your friends and family.
Think only on that perfect gift to all that Jesus came and brought.
The gift of love and life and peace . . . share *that* with all humanity.

Believe that He can do all things for those who do believe
Believe from Him all blessings flow, and believe all things are blessings.
He said He'd prepare a place for you, so to this you must cleave
For it's been told two thousand years and still goes on professing.

The best gift you can ever give is to daily show mankind
The love that child left here on earth does through your actions tell
That you believe His words are true and His light through you does shine.
When you believe that child is love, then through you peace will dwell.

12/24/2016

LIFE . . .

A Caregiver's Prayer
Changes
Cry a River
Daddy's Footsteps
Day by Day
How You Make Me Feel
I Smile
I'm Only a Machine
Let Me Borrow Your Husband
Mekhi and the Sea Turtle
Night Flight
Ode to a Mouse
One More Day
Pity Party
Remembered So
Rescued
Tale of a Puppy's Tail
Three Rings
Today is a Good Day

A CAREGIVER'S PRAYER

Here it is, another day
God give me strength
To make my way
Through pain, disease and sorrow.

You've blessed my mind
Please guide my hands
That unseen veins I somehow find
All skills from you I borrow.

"Nurse, please don't go!"
Is what I hear
"I'm hurt, and filled with so much fear
My death is soon to follow."

I'm trained to care
No time to grieve
There's still more suffering to relieve
God, rest me for tomorrow.

2/7/1996

CHANGES

You took me from my father's house
A child not schooled in life
A bird who knew not it had wings
And made me still your wife.

"An empty slate," is what you said
Upon which you would write
The daily course which I would take
Against which I should not fight.

My lessons, one by one, I'd learn
By your example, book and world
And slowly metamorphed with time
No longer daddy's little girl.

Too busy with the day-to-day
The change I'd yet to see
You told me in so many words
I was no longer me.

Only when you work with clay
The plan in mind when you begin
You shape and mold it every day
And get your vision in the end.

Now hold your bellows, do not pout
I'm not a piece of clay
My wings have just begun to sprout
More changes are on the way!

6/1982

CRY A RIVER

My eyes cry a river from my heart
That floods my very soul
A river that has no earthly end
And has no final goal.

My eyes cry a river that cannot dry
For man does not understand
The plagues that make souls die
Are endless as the sand.

My eyes cry a river that flows through time
Flooding every land and sea
Until we learn that to be kind
Is what we're meant to be.

9/11/1999

DADDY'S FOOTSTEPS

I remember Daddy's footsteps
In the middle of the night
As he paced along the hallways
Awaiting day's first light.

I wondered what disturbed him
As the hours ebbed away
And what could not be pondered
In the passing of the day.

The window seemed to tell him
With its panoramic view
All the answers to his queries
And just what he had to do.

By day his stride much longer
I tried to match with all my might
His giant steps grew shorter
In the shadows of twilight.

And now that I am wiser
I go to my window, too,
For the answers to life's questions
Or just the solace of night's view.

I can but smile as I remember
Daddy's footsteps as I grew
For I now walk in Daddy's footsteps
They've become my footsteps, too.

4/4/1996

DAY BY DAY

Day by day I wake to find
New knowledge bestowed on me
Like a giant puzzle in my mind
Some small piece I'm allowed to see.

Day by day I learn to take
The lesson of that day
Knowing it is no mistake
I chose to go that way.

A perpetual university
I seem enrolled for life
Guiding me through adversity
To minimize all strife.

Day by day as lessons do unravel
I'll tutor new enrollees
To guide their daily travel
With knowledge each one seizes.

So, fret no more on little stuff
For tests will come your way
You can master trials tough
If you take them day by day.

3/13/1996

HOW YOU MAKE ME FEEL

Today I wasn't feeling well.
My problems were great and small.
I needed help so I rang my bell
But you didn't come at all.

So, I got up to help myself.
What else was I to do?
You showed me with ignoring stealth
What to expect from you.

My legs were weak, so I went down
Just as I knew I might.
When you came in, you wore a frown
That hurt me throughout the night.

I think you changed and fed me
And then put me back to bed
I don't remember what you did
Or much of what you said.

I do remember that I cried
To think you didn't care.
It pained more than my silly pride
While I was lying there.

It matters not your assignments
Or if your tasks to you appeal
The thing that matters most to me
Is how you make me feel!

6/24/2008

I SMILE

At night I close my eyes to rest
I'm weary from the day
With worldly woes upon my breast
And sleep so far away.

I think back on those yesterdays
When I was but a child
That you were there just like today
And my heart has to smile.

The tension then begins to ease
Each muscle one by one
Finds relaxation that it needs
Like earth needs setting sun.

A vision of your smiling face
Or how your eyes beguile
Can bring me to my slumber place
And to another smile.

As day breaks through my solitude
I pause for just a while
So thankful just for knowing you
And once again I smile.

4/1973

I'M ONLY A MACHINE

I'm built to be reliable
Give me care and keep me clean
I'll do my very best for you
But I'm only a machine.

See my pretty little lights?
How beautifully they shine
They let you know what's happening
To save you precious time.

Touch my buttons gently
In sequence one by one
Then have faith and trust in me
To get the treatment done.

I'll never second guess you.
I do just as I'm told
Provide sure hands to guide me
And you'll always reach your goal.

I'll give you little warnings
When you're rough or treat me mean
But ask yourself what you did wrong
'Cause I'm only a machine.

10/20/1989

LET ME BORROW YOUR HUSBAND

My dear, let me borrow your husband
For just an hour or two
Don't worry, I swear I'll send him back
And in better spirits, too.

I'll take away his stress and his cares
I'll relax him for a while
I'll never call or disturb you at home
For I'm a diversion with style.

My dear, don't waste time being jealous
Your hours are far better spent
Ensuring his home is his castle
Instead of fretting about where he went.

So, groom and pamper and polish
For never too far will he roam
When no place can make him feel better
Than he does each time he comes home.

My dear, let me borrow your husband!
Let him do as other men do
He'll play cards and be boisterous for hours
And return home more loving to you.

3/23/1996

MEKHI AND THE SEA TURTLE

I watched you grow since you were conceived
Cozy and contented within.
The water broke, your birth not achieved . . .
Defiantly stubborn even then.

My pride and joy, my very first one
No need were you ever denied.
My biggest favorite grandson
Our duty – only to lead and to guide.

Not meant to be a sea turtle
To drive your life messages home.
We tried in ways both stern and subtle
To get you to the day when you were grown.

Sea turtles, you were told, need no guidance
They're laid in the sand in a patch.
With instinct they form an alliance
And race to the sea as they hatch.

No mother to hold or to love them
No father to ward off a shark.
Their future should really be dim
As they stumble and crawl through the dark.

They just know that survival's not assured
On themselves alone they must rely.
So they struggle 'til their safety's secured
For to do less means they surely will die.

Oh how I wish that you were a sea turtle
And life's harshness you knew how to endure.
So that you'd leap over each hurdle
Until you were *really* grown and mature.

Not meant to be this sea creature
Only guidance and rules come your way . . .
Your family, given as the teacher
To keep you from being life's prey.

Take heed of all those boring teachings
That you hated and said made no sense.
As you were dragged through them kicking and screaming
They were to grow you and not cause offense.

To a sound happy life there're no short cuts
It's hard work and takes sage lessons learned.
It takes strength and endurance and guts
And starting over when you get burned.

Don't give up when you get defeated
The wise see the error of their ways.
Don't think that life left you cheated
Then retreat in a smoky grey haze.

Sea turtles aren't snuggled or cuddled
They know no one they can call all their own.
They were hatched in a dark sandy huddle
No kindness or affection were they shown.

Be glad you were born with a parent
And with blessings too numerous to count.
Admit when your actions are errant
So better tactics towards perils you can mount.

Know your friend and know your enemy
Know who will never lead you to wrong.
Look ahead and see your own destiny
Set priorities where they belong.

Charm and good looks will take you just so far
Let integrity and your good word set the pace.
For lies and deceit leaves a heart's scar
And your character in massive disgrace.

Will your actions help or thwart you?
Would you want those you love to know
That this action you're taking just threw you
Into a place you did not mean to go?

Like a sea turtle be sure to strive
For the life you really want to lead.
Assured that you'll more than survive
When guided by sage lessons – you'll succeed.

3/26/2021

NIGHT FLIGHT

Did you ever fly by night
And look out on that lovely sight
Of darkness broken by the light of
Townships everywhere?

And think of all the poverty
That moves amongst prosperity
All over this vast country
Yet hides so well at night?

But it somehow seems to dissipate
This poverty that I so hate
When all those lights look oh so great
When ere I fly by night.

1/27/1978

ODE TO A MOUSE

A scraping, grating, irritating
Noise kept me from sleeping
I tossed and turned; my anger burned
While a mouse resumed housekeeping.

It wasn't that I really cared
About the space that we both shared
But rather that the noise impaired
The needed rest that could not be spared.

At one o'clock, then two, then three
She ran from drawer to closet
"What is she doing? Get up and see?"
That's when my husband lost it!

"Have you gone mad or lost your head
That you'd disturb my rest
Just to get me out of bed
To look for some mouse's nest!?!"

"Go back to sleep and shut your yap
And just leave me alone
If you insist, I'll set a trap
The thing just wants a home!"

A HOME?! I shuddered at the thought
Of sisters, brothers, cousins
All leaving evidence about
Of banquets, hikes and love-ins!

And when the trap lay full with bait
My protector and defender
Condemned me as I sat to wait
To hear the sentence rendered.

At last the snap of closing trap
Was heard throughout the house
Consumed by joy I had to clap
To be rid of that pesky mouse.

No sisters, brothers, cousins
Multiplying here and there
No disgusting evidence to clean
Or look for everywhere.

Then my protector and defender
Thought it only fair to show
The limp and mangled body
Of the mouse that had to go.

Oh, GOD! I thought I'd really die
As the carcass was brought in
I guess to order it put to death
Was some sort of mortal sin.

Everyone said I was a louse
To kill this tiny little mouse
Who only wanted a nice warm house
To raise her family in.

A little tear ran down my face
As I looked upon the lonely place
The mouse had thought would be her space
  To romp and play and live in.

Some crumpled here and there
Some in a shoe I did not wear
The space I truly had to spare
  If I wasn't so neurotic.

Oh mouse, I guess I must now confess
  You didn't make so big a mess
  I should have cared a little less
  And now I'm really sorry!

I hope this puts you more at rest
  To know I'll try my very best
  To see a mouse as less a pest
  When next we do encounter.

Oh no! There's that scraping, grating, irritating
  Noise that kept me from sleeping!
  I'll toss and turn, but no anger burns
  Oh mouse, resume housekeeping.

(Tomorrow I'll get a cat!)

5/6/1993

ONE MORE DAY

When you're tired, pushing burnout
In your bed you'd rather stay
Can't think of any reason
To go through another day.

When you've lost all motivation
Frustrations cloud your view
Think you need a brand-new challenge
And your Pepsi just won't do.

Get a grip, then take a cleansing breath
Think who the effort's for
Humanity is waiting
So, step spryly out your door.

"The force" is there to help you
Push those clouds of doubt away
The world will surely thank you
'Cause you made it one more day.

10/12/1989

PITY PARTY

I have spent far too much time
At pity parties drunk of wine
Alone without a true friend to find
To join me in my sorrow.

Everyday a new-found woe
Bids me to certain bottles go
For mock strength to fight a hidden foe
Yet rise renewed tomorrow.

Never did I ever see
The monster there defeating me
Had no intent to set me free
Hell bent to leave me hollow.

Surely it was not my fate
To merely sit and contemplate
More misery without real escape
When change in luck must follow.

Now be gone you hellish fiend
Release this soul on which you feed
No further contempt here will you breed
New faith I've found to borrow.

For always with the new day
My troubles weak can never stay
If service to mankind I will pay
And arrogance I swallow.

Pity Party, good riddance!
Your ghost can no longer menace
With my dictum,
Amicus Humani Generis
("friend to the human race")
No more in you I'll wallow.

8/27/2009

REMEMBERED SO

He lost himself in yesterday
Unable to correct
Mistakes that his freewill had made
That filled him with regret.

And as a new year starts again
He finds he must decide
If he should trounce the mundane
Or just give up, lie down, and die.

God knows, he's truly tired
He's weary to the bone
Nothing is the way he planned
He wants to just go home.

No good to those around him
Not even to himself
Withdrawn from friends who love him
His talents stored on a shelf.

Was he to be remembered so . . .
Withdrawn, alone, and miffed
With self-esteem rock-bottom low
The future all adrift?

Well, that can't be his epitaph
His descendants would be pained
When gazing 'pon his photograph
Baring melancholy unexplained.

No cause to wallow in shades of blue
No earthly needs had he
Perhaps not thought completely through
No longer melancholy would he be.

Uplift others and not himself alone
To please, would be his pleasure
Kind thoughts are grown from good seeds sown
In heaping, hearty measure.
He'd count his blessings, as they were many
And cheer himself in knowing
His gifts he'd share – some haven't plenty
Then note his own bliss growing.

For it is said, and he'd find it true
That as your gifts to others flow
In kindness folks upon you view
And you'll be remembered so.

1/1984

RESCUED

New, fragile, no independent power
A babe in arms for sure
To bathe, to nurture by the hour
With breaks and braces to endure.

Oddly through this little leech
Nature makes our life skewed
That someone must extend their reach
So this little life can be rescued.

They come to be with so much need
Enough to make one smother
Yet can find a way to plant that seed
That transforms a girl into a mother.

As time goes by dependence fades;
Little more can you impart
Out of braces, out of braids
but never out of your heart.

Now they too have their own cares
as every day's a challenge
Committed to their own affairs
Not knowing how they'll manage.

But stop they do, as you have done
Sacrificing all they can
Turning tables have begun
As by your side they stand.

Old and fragile, slowly losing power
From one loss to the other
They hover, and nurture a fading flower
As they now become the mother.

Once reality has soaked in
And the ego's more subdued
You're grateful knowing that you win
('Fore your child has come)
And alas, you've been rescued.

2/8/2015

TALE OF A PUPPY'S TAIL

The story you are about to read is true. The names haven't been changed to protect anybody! The guilty are guilty and the innocent are just young. Age slowly!

Some puppies have a lot of tail
While others haven't any.
Some tails are short and all puffed out
And some are long and skinny.

I used to think it must be sad
To be without a tail.
But don't feel sad for those without
Come listen to my tale.

I used to have a flowing tail
It dragged along the ground.
I'd trip up little kitty cats
And watch them tumble down.

My name is Josie
And I'm a pup who loved to run and play
Until I had a strange mishap
Or a cold December day.

Just running in and out of doors . . .
My master called to me,
"Come back, be careful, stay inside!"
But I just had to be free.

Sooo, out the door and down the steps
I hadn't gone too far,
When suddenly to my surprise
I was hit by a speeding car.

The city ought to post a sign . . .
"Puppies Out To Play!
Just Slow Down!
Don't Go So Fast!
Wild Puppies Out Today!"

Too proud to yelp or holler
Tail tucked between my legs
I tried to sneak back in the house
Behind my master's head.

She knew there was a problem
From the way I hung my head.
She rushed right in to help me
And put me in my bed.

My master lifted up my tail
But it fell right back down!
Nothing she did could keep it up
And she gave me a causative frown.

She didn't try to scold me
Though she wanted to, I bet.
Instead, she sat and told me
She would take me to the vet.

Some vets are forgotten soldiers
Left over from some war.
Other vets are real fast cars
You ride in to the store.

Well, this vet, my master said
Was not a car or soldier.
She explained this was a puppy's doc
As she rubbed me on my shoulder.

Well, just my luck,
This vet was stranger than anything
that happened that day.
The doc just sewed and wrapped me up . . .
My master had nothing to say.

The scary thing that happened next
Would even make you holler!
My master helped to hold me still
While they put on this G-I-A-N-T collar.

Now I don't mean a stylish one
With rhinestones, baubles or lace.
This thing was sure to make me look
Like the DOG FROM OUTER SPACE!!!
(And it did, too!)

I couldn't see to left or right
Only what was straight ahead.
My friends all thought a lost spaceship
Had landed on my head.

Some thought that it was funny
They laughed until they cried.
Others ran and hid with fear
While I just felt dumb inside.

This collar should have done some good
To keep me from pulling at my tail.
I surely couldn't have been sadder
If they'd locked me up in jail.

"No, Jo, no!", my master shouted
Whenever I tried to break free.
She said it was for my own good
But it didn't seem like that to me.

I'm sure that you can understand
Why this collar had to go.
The thing just seemed to cramp my style
And . . . it made me go too slow!

I couldn't fit through the doggy door.
When I was out, I was out.
But horror of all horrors, when I was in . . .
I couldn't get out again!

My doggy pals wouldn't come to play
They thought I was contagious.
Why, if they had just half a brain
They'd know that was outrageous!

My tail was really quite a mess
It wouldn't wag or wave.
Just sort of drooped and dragged along . . .
The situation was most grave.

What could be done to cure my plight?
My tail just wouldn't heal.
Would I forever be this sight
That made little children squeal?

This wasn't some sort of fashion statement!
It was never going to be chic.
I'd never make the center fold
Of *Puppy of the Week*!
I knew just what I had to do
To regain my respect and reputation.
There was one chance for me to cure
This tail-and-collar situation.

From the corner of my eye
I saw sitting all alone
A little boy so sad and shy
Like he'd just lost his home.

So, I walked over to this lad
And asked what was his plight.
Thought I'd cheer him up since he was sad
That's when he told me about his kite.

It seems while playing with the boys
His kite had lost its tail.
It went up and dove right back down.
The strong winter wind could not make it sail.

"My son, my son," I'm sure I said,
"I can ensure your kite will sail."
A plan forming in my head . . .
"I only ask assistance with my problematic tail."

As he slowly looked around
I thought that he'd 'bout drop dead
While I assured and calmed him down
About that spaceship on my head.

Then he collected his composure
And came just a little closer
Asking what could be my proposal
To give his kite its flight.

"Why it is you who'd do me the favor
And free me of this blight
If you'd use my tail as the sailer
For your kite."

"As a tail for me it is a nuisance.
With it I can no longer fight
But I'm sure it still has uses
As a tail to sail your kite."

As we thought we'd help each other
I told him of a plan I thought we'd try
To solve the problems of one another
And he dried each weeping eye.

The dear fellow moved in closer
Undid the snaps that held the collar tight
Freeing my head and shoulder
From that flying-saucer sight.

I felt like a brand-new puppy
Free at last to run and play
No longer sad and grumpy
But first there was a debt I had to pay.

So, I turned my head around
And with precision, I must say
Popped that tail onto the ground
Where most useless it did lay.

And then tying it real tight
We affixed it to his kite
And both watched while it took flight
As the wind took it away.

Well, the little boy was happy
But, not half as much as I.
No longer feeling crappy
As we watched our tail fly high.

Though I cannot trip a kitty
There's no need to show me pity
For my tail that isn't long.
Just smile when you see kites flying strong.

1991

THREE RINGS

Three rings have come into my life
That have brought me to today
Each with a magnetism
That sustains me when I sway.

The first, was quite remarkable
Perfected with a flaw
Visible on close inspection
That through a frozen heart could gnaw.

The giver most distressed
When learning of that state
The recipient saw pure beauty
As the reality of her mate.

Real without pretension
Strong in every way
True to his convictions
Who would keep the world at bay.

Dismayed by imperfection
An "upgrade" then was made
Perfect, grander, larger
Upon her finger laid.

She wore it since it pleased him
Yet its predecessor's glow
Held a stronger, truer meaning
Than the giver could ever know.

Ring three, just seen in passing
Holds a special meaning still
Holding fast the love of others
With commitment and strong will.

I've gazed on it with wonder
It does my spirit good
To see an everlasting bond
That through life's trials stood.

As the second cannot replace the first
Whose station is so secured
The third, too, irreplaceable
Its meaning through eternity ensured.

10/21/2017

TODAY IS A GOOD DAY

Today is a good day
Though mine be filled with tears
For the times we'll not have together
For the end of future years.

Today is a good day
Because I knew you well
You were the very heart of me
That pushed me to excel.

Today is a good day
As every day will be
In tears or laughter eternally
Because you walked with me.

Today is a good day
Though mine begins in tears
For the times of joy and sadness
I've felt throughout the years.

Today . . . another good day
No matter what the end
Because I can smile in knowing
You'll always be my friend.

11/19/2013

• • •

A Friend Responds

Today is a good day
With the sunshine of love
Streaming through the windows of the soul
Turning tears to glistening diamonds
Falling gently on pillows of
Hope
Love
Joy
and
Ultimate Peace.

11/19/2013

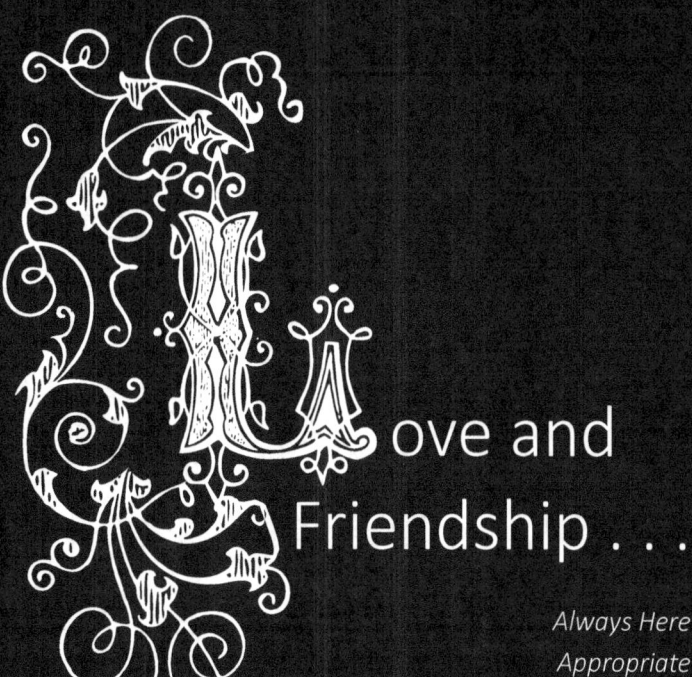

Love and Friendship...

Always Here
Appropriate
Emotion
For You Have Seen
Friend
If Time Stood Still
Proclivity Component
Should I?
The Care Package
The Gladiola
The Single Tear
Until
You Don't
Your Eyes
Your Star

ALWAYS HERE

Lovers leave each other
Friends never do.
Just be here when I need you
I'm always here for you.

4/1997

APPROPRIATE

He smiles while softly telling me,
"You can always make me stop to think of something nice."
Then says, "It's inappropriate!"
When reflecting on it twice.

"INAPPROPRIATE"?
I pondered at a loss.
That surely cannot be
For no such word could ever exist
Between this man and me.

I like his nerve!
To stir me so
And then to drop me flat
A Scorpio left wondering
Just what he meant by that.

But never will I be outdone
In games of love or chance
To flirt was his catastrophe
When he laid his insidious plans
To test this female's curiosity.

Were I the sort of teasing girl
That many others seem to be
I'd tell him how his kisses taste
Or how my heart pounds to the touch
Of his breath upon my face.

I'd much rather show him where the buttons are
That set my libido purring
And our passions will authenticate
Our passage through that moment
But when the time is more appropriate.

5/8/1992

EMOTION

There you are, and here I am
Emotive both are we
Attempting to unveil the truth...
Man's true identity.

Emotion is the sort of stuff
That seems to transcend fact,
But with the help of intellect
We can endorse this simple pact . . .

To allow our greater intellect
To control emotive strife,
To be we all responsible
For our actions throughout life.

5/1981

FOR YOU HAVE SEEN

For you have seen the best of me
And the worse of me alike
You've seen me at the end of day
And in the predawn light.

With no bridge to hold you
Nor lass to sway your will
You go when you have need to
Yet returning to me still.

For you have seen the soul of me
That most will never know
The good, the bad, and yes, faux me
Yet something holds you so.

Now when I ponder on my life
You appear in every scene
In awe am I, that you're still here
Despite all that you have seen.

6/14/2013

FRIEND

Teach me that which I don't know
Light the path where I must go
Encourage me when I must bend
Throughout my life, remain my friend.

Praise me when I do achieve
Sigh with me when ere I grieve
When down and out, be there to lend
Throughout my life, remain my friend.

Content will be my short stay here
With thoughts of you so very dear
Peace will rest me at my end
Knowing that I called you friend.

2/26/1992

IF TIME STOOD STILL

If time stood still for you and me
How very happy I could be
To spend each day and every night
To bask and grow in your love's light
If time could just stand still.

If time stood still for you and me
We'd spend our whole eternity
In peace and love and harmony
Without possessive jealously
If time could just stand still.

If time stood still for you and me
There'd be no pain or poverty
To sadden our spirits
If time could just stand still.

If time stood still for you and me
We'd be young forever
With no pain or infirmity
To interfere with our spirits
If time could just stand still.

But alas, time cannot stand still for you or me
We live with fear and worry constantly
That life we'll not control.
So, just for this moment here and now
Let's make our hearts stand still.

7/16/1995

PROCLIVITY COMPONENT

Come and lay here by my side
There are things that you should know
Things of which I'll all deny
'Less sparkling waters flow.

My heart is heavy, my head confused
No sleep to set me free
Most days to dreaming do I lose
Since you can't be with me.

Too sad to think that you and I
So perfect for each other
Commitment bound to live a lie
Protecting yet another.

What cruel quirk of nature lives
In only up-right beasts
That one just takes, and one just gives
While making his needs least?

I'll tell you truest friend of friends
No matter what our fate
In spite of all the curves life sends
You are my one true mate.

Though circumstances may bind us
To decisions made in haste
No man-made morals restrict us
From a love we must not waste.

So, come and lay here by my side
For one last stolen moment
Too much alike our souls to hide
Our proclivity component.

5/6/1993

SHOULD I?

Should I look deep into your eyes
For warm affection there?
Or should I simply look away
Pretending not to care?

Should I let you hold my hand
As friends will often do?
Should I find comfort in your arms
Like I've always wanted to?

Should I let you kiss my lips?
Should I respond in kind?
Should I ignore my pounding heart
And pacify my mind?

Should I fortify my mortal frame
With daily food and drink?
Should I breathe another breath?
On these things I need not think!

Convention held my spirit long
Suppressed for the common good.
My soul wants now to live again
My heart knows that it could.

To live this life another day
I say to you I would.
To give expression to my love
One answer, yes, I should.

5/9/2018

THE CARE PACKAGE

If we could, we'd give you
A house down by the shore
And that shiny brand-new SUV
That you've been wishing for.

If we could, we'd give you
A business you would run
So you could work the way you want
Or just show up for fun.

Since we have not money
A fact you know is true
This little "Care Package" from our hearts
Will sort of have to do.

Though it be belated
Our love for you is not
As God gave the world all that He had
We give you what we've got . . .

All our love for every season
And just for no good reason

By Mom and Dad

12/25/2008

THE GLADIOLA

The gladiola springs a bud
Upon a strong tall stem
It opens in the sun and rain
Its glow is never dim.

Its full intent is pleasing
It gives color and delight
Its beauty shows in morning
Yet it blooms all through the night.

It never minds the rains of spring
Nor the heated suns of summer
And autumn leaves and winter snows
Just give it time for slumber.

With every year the buds loom forth
New beauty to deliver
With very little care at all
Why should the gardener consider . . .

That maybe little gladiola
In old and weathered soil
Now needs a little TLC
To make her stems stay tall?

To give the blossoms brighter color?
To spring forth little suckers?
To keep his garden free from clutter?
So his gladiola doesn't suffer.

The loving, tender gardener
Tried as best he thought he could
To lessen gladiola's work
Of making his garden look good.

As he started on new projects
Other flowers gave him delight
His gladiola withered
'Neath shaded, filtered light.
The blossoms slowly lost their glow
The stem grew weak and small
But the gardener never noticed
With his shrubs and plants and all.

Then one spring after many years
The garden seemed most bare
There were roses, pansies, daffodils
But his gladiola wasn't there!

The gardener sat and pondered
Why his faithful blossom died
For she, above all others,
Was his beauty and his pride.

Hadn't he pruned and clipped and weeded?
Hadn't he raked and plowed and seeded?
Always sweating, aching, bleeding!
What more could she be needing?

The gardener wept and cried,
"I did my best – I tried,
I lightened gladiola's duty
To give my garden beauty
And still she died!"

A butterfly was passing through
And told the gardener not to cry.
"I think that I can help you,
If you will sit and listen why."

"Help me," said he,
"What do you know –
My gladiola just won't grow.
She's dead," he said, then dropped down to his knee.

The butterfly just shook her head
"Your gladiola isn't dead –
Why don't you fertilize her bed?
She's only in a coma!"

The gardener sprang up singing
"A coma! What is your meaning?"
The butterfly just flew away
And left the gardener thinking.

At last it did to him occur
That what he gave his gladiola
Were things to him most pleasing
Not what was best for her.

Now could he labor just as hard
To revive her from her coma?
Could the gardener restore his yard?
Could he get back his gladiola?

He took down all the towering trees
That shaded out the light.
He thinned out all that grew from seeds
Then fertilized just right.

The gardener kept his daily watch
He watered and he prayed
He vowed he'd always feed her
If her life would just be saved.

And then one day in early spring
The ground it broke and bore
A tiny gladiola sprout
But there was nothing more.

No long, tall stem nor blossom
Would shoot up from the ground
The wary gladiola sighed
"I'm afraid you'll let me down.

You might forget to fertilize!
You might want other flowers!
You might go off and leave me here
For hours and hours and hours!"

The gardener begged and pleaded.
He would take the time to care
He would be sure to consider
What the gladiola thought was fair.

Today, the happy gardener's bed
Is brilliant, blooming over.
His selfish nature gladly shed
To keep his gladiola.

5/31/1988

THE SINGLE TEAR

When life has done all it could to you
When you have fought your level best
When the future, like glass, is clearly in view
When there's nothing more to confess

Then you can stop and look at the world
And all that you are leaving behind
With your every deed before you unfurled
When you know them to be pure and kind

When you look through the soul of your love
When you know this dimension will pass
When no world expresses the content thereof
When no human deed has power at last

When there is nothing on earth more to fear
Then give the world your final goodbye
Give your best again with one final tear
When this life you at long last defy

There was nothing more precious you gave
There's no jewel or diamond more clear
Than the meaning, wordless, flouting the grave
Than your love in that last final tear.

For Lloyd George Washington
6/13/1969 – 3/23/2012 and forever!

3/20/2012

UNTIL

Until there is no memory

Of these events gone by

Until there is not sun or moon

Or stars to light the sky.

Until the beach has no more sand

Until the winds don't blow

Until the day beyond all time

Our love can only grow.

So, meet me at the edge of time

To go with me from there

Beyond all eternity

Until . . .

7/31/1999

YOU DON'T

you don't have to be alone
TO BE LONELY

you don't have to have tears
TO CRY

you don't have to starve
TO BE HUNGRY

and you don't have to be dead
TO DIE.

11/18/2012

YOUR EYES

Love me always with your eyes
Adore me in a crowded room
Tell me just how much you need me
In your guitar's yearning tune.

Brush me as you pass me by
Let me sense you in the air
Jar my deepest daydreams of you
With your sudden presence there.

Too soon again you'll leave me
Too soon again I'll realize
All I really do have of you
Is the loving from your eyes.

11/24/2000

YOUR STAR

My son, the day you came the sky was bright
Your parents so grateful and proud
For you we'd prayed with all our might
You were perfect with lungs so loud.

You've grown to be the man you are
Marching to a drum all your own
Guided by your created star
That still shines bright for you alone.

12/18/2020

ABOUT THE POETESS

Gladys Lois Washington (née Felder) was born an "army brat" in 1948 in Fort Lee Virginia. As the eldest of five daughters, she always had plenty to say, but to maintain decorum expected of children growing up in that era, to express feelings that might otherwise be considered rude or disrespectful, she found pen and paper, and writing to herself, a more acceptable form of expression than yelling in a closet or waiting for exactly the right word to surface in a conversation in which she was engaged.

The death of her mother, Frankie Roberta Felder, at the age of thirty-three when Gladys was twelve, began a lifetime of deep thoughts and sleepless nights. A lited image of a cross through a full moon in the pre-dawn hours upon her mother's death was the catalyst for her analysis of poetry and poets' intentions – their use of given words, their meanings and the inspirations. The image of that cross "spoke" to her – not in words – but in feelings. Unexpressed feelings and thoughts that kept her awake at night.

Sixty-two years later, this light-sleeping deep thinker keeps her pen and paper resting at her bedside – if not in the bed with her – always prepared to jot down "jagged thoughts, often barely legible in daylight" that might become the substance of future poems.

Gladys lives and writes in sunny Florida where she and her husband, Lloyd, raised their three children. She now spends the rest of her time being Nana to six grandchildren and traveling the world with family and friends.

www.ingramcontent.com/pod-product-compliance
Lightning Source LLC
Chambersburg PA
CBHW071348080526
44587CB00017B/3013